PLATFORM PAPERS

QUARTERLY ESSAYS ON THE PERFORMING ARTS

No. 33
October 2012

CURRENCY HOUSE

Changing Times at NIDA

CHRIS PUPLICK

PLATFORM PAPERS
Quarterly essays from Currency House Inc.

Founding Editor: Dr John Golder

Currency House Inc. is a non-profit association and resource centre advocating the role of the performing arts in public life by research, debate and publication.
Postal address: PO Box 2270, Strawberry Hills, NSW 2012, Australia
Email: info@currencyhouse.org.au   Tel: (02) 9319 4953
Website: www.currencyhouse.org.au   Fax: (02) 9319 3649
Editorial Board: Katharine Brisbane AM, Michael Campbell, Dr John Golder, John McCallum, Martin Portus, Greig Tillotson

Changing Times at NIDA © Chris Puplick 2012

ISBN 978 0 9872114 2 2
ISSN 1449-583X
Typeset in 10.5 Arrus BT
Printed by Ligare Book Printers, Riverwood, NSW
This edition of Platform Papers is supported by the Sidney Myer Fund, Neil Armfield, David Marr, Joanna Murray-Smith, Martin Portus, Janne Ryan, Alan Seymour and other individual donors and advisers. To them and to all our supporters Currency House extends sincere gratitude.

SIDNEY MYER FUND

Contents

AVAILABILITY *Platform Papers*, quarterly essays
on the performing arts, is published every January,
April, July and October and is available through
bookshops or by subscription. For order form,
please visit www.currencyhouse.org.au

LETTERS Currency House invites readers to
submit letters of 400–1,000 words in response
to the essays. Letters should be emailed to the
Editor at info@currencyhouse.org.au or posted
to Currency House at PO Box 2270, Strawberry
Hills, NSW 2012, Australia. To be considered for
the next issue, the letters must be received by
15 November.

CURRENCY HOUSE For membership details, see
our website at: www.currencyhouse.org.au

The author

CHRIS PUPLICK, AM has had a distinguished career in public service and support of the arts. After graduating from Sydney University, where he majored in history and political science, he became deeply involved in politics and served as a Liberal Senator for NSW 1978–81 and 1984–90. During that period he was Shadow Minister for Environment, Heritage and the Arts and Manager of Opposition Business in the Senate. He was also Secretary of the Parliamentary Branch of Amnesty International.

After leaving Parliament he pursued a career first as an environmental consultant and subsequently as President of the NSW Anti-Discrimination Board and as the first NSW Privacy Commissioner. During this period he was also Chair of the Central Sydney Area Health Service, the AIDS Trust of Australia and the Australian National Council on AIDS, Hepatitis C and Related Diseases and was a member of the Zoological Parks Board. He conducted several public inquiries in areas as diverse as reviewing Australia's policies on international whaling controls and the use of electronic health records; and represented Australia in several international forums including the International Whaling Commission and the United Nations General Assembly. He has a particular interest in public health policy and currently serves on the Board of Justice Health.

In the arts area he served as a Trustee of the Australian Museum, chair of the Griffin Theatre and Freelance Dance Company; and for three years the

Theatre Board of the Australia Council. He was a Board member of NIDA 1994–2000 and 2007–10. From 2008–12 he was the inaugural Chair of the National Film and Sound Archive of Australia. He has published five books and numerous journal articles including Platform Paper no.18 (2007): *Getting Heard: Achieving an Effective Arts Advocacy*. He was awarded membership in the Order of Australia for his services to social justice and leadership in the HIV/AIDS advocacy field.

Acknowledgements

My thanks to Katharine Brisbane, Mark Williams and others at Currency House for the invitation to write this second Platform Paper and for the chance to get a great deal off my chest. I am deeply grateful to many people in both the wider theatre community and in the NIDA fraternity for their generosity in encouraging me to write this paper. I have interviewed dozens of members of NIDA staff, Board members and students both past and present and I particularly wish to thank those people who have allowed me to use details of their personal experience at NIDA in this publication. There were many others who, for a variety of reasons, preferred that their names or circumstances not be canvassed and I have respected their wishes. Although I was unable to interview either the current Director or Chair of NIDA, I was able to talk with Jeff Janisheski, the new Head of Acting, and I appreciate how open he was with me in that conversation. I wish him well in his difficult task.

Introduction

Changing Times at NIDA is the third Platform Paper to examine the tergiversations of a major Australian performing or teaching arts institution. James Waites' *Whatever Happened to the STC Actors Company?* traced the establishment, growth, flowering and eventual collapse of an innovative ensemble initiated by the Sydney Theatre Company as a model for experimental theatre making.[1] Richard Murphet's *The Fall and Rise of the VCA* examined how the Victorian College of the Arts, a highly-regarded and well-established arts education and training institution, fell upon hard times, saw its previous excellent reputation tarnished if not trashed, was forced to rethink its fundamental purposes and practices and emerged from the ordeal a strong and better institution.[2]

This paper will focus on the National Institute of Dramatic Art (NIDA), long regarded as Australia's premier theatre training school, and is both an investigation and a protest. It examines a number of questions such as why a new administration at NIDA (both at the level of a new Artistic Director and a compliant Board) has appeared so anxious to distance itself from the history of NIDA under the leadership of John Clark and Elizabeth Butcher who, for the better part of forty years, built NIDA into a position of pre-eminence; and to systematically rid itself of all the leading teachers and staff associated with that period. Was it just the need for change?

It will examine why, in terms of NIDA's reputation, a point could be reached that a self-survey of 50 Acting Students in 2011 could yield an 84% affirmative response to the question: *'Are you worried about the reputation of NIDA declining in the professional community?'*

It will interrogate the process by which an Artistic Director was appointed to the nation's premier theatre training school with no experience or qualifications as a professional acting teacher, director or playwright, and whose knowledge of contemporary Australian writing or theatre production was almost non-existent after a period of a quarter of a century living outside Australia; and how her determination to corporatize NIDA and to replace its 'dysfunctional' Acting Department (her terminology) under the rubric of 'creative transformation'[3] has transformed the very nature of NIDA itself.

It will outline the processes by which nearly all of NIDA's senior staff were pushed, squeezed or, as at least one claimed, bullied out of NIDA; and how this led eventually to the appointment of an American Head of Acting who, despite his undoubted qualities as a teacher, has no background knowledge or direct experience of Australian theatre, culture or teaching philosophies and practices.

In his paper, Richard Murphet describes his membership of VCA staff and participation in many of the events he reports:

> *I should say at the outset that this essay is not research of solely historical interest [...] In yet another disclaimer I abjure any degree of objectivity in my overview.*[4]

I make the same disclaimer. From 2007 until 2010 I was a member of the NIDA Board—my second period, having served from 1991 to 1996. I opposed the appointment of Lynne Williams as Artistic Director and was eventually asked to leave the Board by the Chairman, Malcolm Long,[5] who found my role as a 'dissident director' unacceptable. More of that anon.

It is natural, indeed inevitable, that after forty years under one educational paradigm and administrative regime, any institution must address the fundamental questions: are we keeping up with the times, is our model still relevant, is now the appropriate (perhaps only) time to undertake fundamental root and branch changes? That in turn requires a sober assessment of the most important question to be addressed by any successful organisation: is our success based on more than simply the brand/reputation or the current personnel? Or is it a consequence of the continuing validity of our philosophies and practices? The answer to this allows decisions to be made about what should (or should not) be changed. Such dilemmas are faced every day in every competitive market place. Remember how, in 1985, one of the most successful companies of all time, the Coca-Cola Company, blundered into a campaign designed to change the taste and image of an iconic product? And was rescued only when, in panic and under pressure, they resolved to restore classic Coke and invest in campaigns to strengthen the fundamental product which had given them world dominance?[6] The current situation at NIDA is like that: a new regime has, I believe, misunderstood both the product and the market and failed to appreciate the basis upon which reputation and success has been built.

To help me understand the positions taken by the current NIDA management, I wrote to the Director seeking to interview her at her convenience. Ms Williams declined to be interviewed. Rather than let the matter rest, I submitted three questions along the above lines to her and invited a written response explaining her position and in particular asking her what she meant by 'creative transformation'. Again, Ms Williams declined and instead referred me to previous NIDA *Annual Reports* and issues of *NIDA News*, along with the *Australian Universities Quality Assessment Report 2010*. I regret this refusal since I am sure that her direct input to this paper would have helped to alleviate my concerns. However, she agreed to my interviewing Jeff Janisheski, the newly appointed Head of Acting, which I found most useful, and she confirmed details of the independent review of the acting course. The documents to which I was referred have provided the basis for some of the conclusions drawn. A similar request to Chairman Malcolm Long was also declined and when I sought access to the minutes and related papers of the Board covering the period I was a Director, the Company Secretary refused my request.

This paper is critical of the current regime at NIDA in relation to a perceived lack of rigour in its pedagogical approach to education and training; its failure to recognise and capitalise upon the extraordinary skills of its long-term staff; and its almost complete failure to engage with either Indigenous culture or with developments in Asia and our region. It has been written because I have a passionate commitment to NIDA and the ideals that have shaped a great institution—ones which I believe are now in peril. I stand by what I have written in terms of the factual basis of my work and I leave others to agree or disagree with the conclusions and prescriptions I draw.

1

A brief history of NIDA

Prior to the mid-1950s there was little or no professional acting or theatre training in Australia, most education being provided privately by individual teachers—mainly English expatriates.[7] The lack of academic regard for Australian writing until the middle of the century was captured by Professor J. I. M. Stewart's much-quoted introduction to his 1940 Commonwealth Literary Fund lectures:

> *I am most grateful to the CLF for providing the funds to give these lectures in Australian literature, but unfortunately they have neglected to provide any literature—I will lecture therefore on D.H. Lawrence's* Kangaroo.[8]

This disdain extended to the performing arts. The University of New South Wales was then in its infancy and its first Vice Chancellor, Philip Baxter, took a more 'modern' view when approached by the Australian Elizabethan Theatre Trust to establish a national acting school on campus. Guided by the newly-appointed professor of Drama, Robert Quentin, Baxter welcomed the opportunity but only after Melbourne University had pronounced it an unfit undertaking for a university.

NIDA was established in 1958 and began teaching in 1959 with Quentin as its foundation Director. Their first home was in a building known as the 'White House' and they initially offered a single course in Acting for 23 students with two full-time staff.

The founding of the school was soon followed by the opening of an associated professional theatre company in a corrugated-iron army mess hall built during World War II. The UNSW had allowed NIDA to convert the hall into a 120-seat theatre and in February 1963 the Old Tote Theatre Company moved in. The company's presence enabled the students to watch the rehearsal process and, in time, to participate. By 1969 the Old Tote had its own theatre and the tin shed became the NIDA Theatre. From 1966 to 1981 NIDA also presented many of its plays at the Jane Street Theatre, another converted hall, in Randwick.

Quentin's vision was to 'develop a distinctly Australian style of acting based on the natural vigour of the students', noting that Australian actors 'had lived too long in the shadow of English understatement'.[9] More will be said about the 'Australian style' of acting and theatre training—a matter of some importance in the light of the recent appointment of NIDA's first non-Australian Head of Acting.

Over the course of the next fifty years NIDA established a variety of courses including Production, Design, Direction, Theatre Crafts, Voice, Movement, Production Management, Playwriting, Costume, Properties and Technical Production. Diplomas were converted into university degrees and a conversion program was established for diploma holders to upgrade in accordance with standards set by NIDA and UNSW.

NIDA's summer schools (beginning 1992) led to the establishment of an Open Program which became an integral part of NIDA's activities and, under the direction of Dr Amanda Morris, a major source of funding. In 2003 a part of that initiative which specialised in Corporate Performance (focussed on business clients) became a separate unit. The 2011 *Annual Report* reveals that in 2010 the Open and Corporate programs between them provided NIDA with income of $5.7 million, some 33% of its total revenues for the year, the remainder largely being provided by the Federal Government.[10]

Quentin's vision, stressing the need to produce 'Australian' actors and to champion Australian works, was taken up by his successor Tom Brown (Director 1963–68) who had studied with the French acting theorist Michel Saint-Denis. In 1969 the turning point came with the appointment of John Clark as its third Director. Almost his first act was to appoint Elizabeth Butcher as Bursar and subsequently General Manager. Thus began the most extraordinary partnership in Australian theatre history—one which was to last forty years and would build NIDA into a national institution and have a profound influence on the Australian theatre and its ancillary industries.

Clark's legacy should be the subject of separate and detailed appreciation. Suffice to say that under his guidance both as a teacher and a director NIDA flourished (although not without a few passing crises, including a notorious student 'strike' in the 1980s); and testimony is to be found both in the honour role of NIDA graduates and the quality of the teaching staff he attracted. A champion both of the classics and of new Australian work, he brought an exceptional intellectual vigour to the institution and created a climate of learning to which all later Australian acting schools have since aspired.

The partnership with Butcher's financial and political stewardship secured its long-term funding in the dark times of the 1980s and oversaw the construction of the spectacular NIDA building, custom-designed as a theatre school and performance space, which opened in October 2001. The respect in which Butcher was held is reflected in her appointment as Chair of the Australia Council Theatre Board and the Sydney Opera House and as the NSW Government's chosen advisor on the establishment in 1979 of the Sydney Theatre Company. It was largely due to her political acuity that NIDA was spared from amalgamation with a university under the Dawkins 'reforms' of the mid-1980s and more recently escaped the fate of other theatre training schools such as the Western Australian Academy of Performing Arts (WAAPA) and the VCA.

Under David Gonski's chairmanship Clark retired in 2004 and was succeeded by Aubrey Mellor, himself a NIDA graduate and former teacher, and one of Australia's most experienced theatre directors and company artistic directors having headed in turn Jane Street, Nimrod, Queensland Theatre Company and Playbox. His background was in variety and circus with training as a dancer and musician; hence he brought to NIDA a view of the need to strengthen the physicality of actors and give them a more robust approach to their work. He used his 1972 Churchill

Fellowship to become the first Australian to undertake a serious study of Asian theatre. Following Mellor's appointment Gonski retired from the Chair to take up the chancellorship of UNSW. Jillian Broadbent briefly replaced him, succeeded by Malcolm Long, then Executive Director of the Australian Film Television and Radio School. NIDA began to see the first hints of the change.

Mellor's tenure as Director was short, lasting only until 2007 and was effectively terminated as a result of his losing the confidence of the Chairman. Mellor had previously complained to Broadbent about what he saw as a lack of direction from the Board, its 'secretive' nature and its lack of engagement with him and respect for his professionalism.[11]

Long's criticisms of Mellor's performance related primarily to a perceived weakness as an administrator and an alleged failure to give the school a strong sense of direction. These concerns were shared by many members of the NIDA staff. What was never called into question were Mellor's skills and ability as a teacher and director. When rumours circulated that his position as Director was not to be renewed a vigorous campaign of luminary graduates such as Cate Blanchett was mounted to save him.[12] In the event, they were not heard.

Butcher's impending departure, announced in the wake of Clark's (and finally taken in 2007) then gave Chairman Long and the NIDA Board the opportunity to restructure the entire administration. Drawing on recent developments at the Royal Academy of Dramatic Art (RADA), the Board, with very little discussion, resolved to amalgamate the positions of Artistic Director and General Manager and to recruit a single person into these two fundamentally different jobs. That decision was, in my view, the most disastrous mistake ever made by NIDA. I do not believe that two such separate and distinct roles can be fulfilled by one person as they require skills which are entirely different and at times actually divergent. The decision deeply divided the NIDA Board and led eventually to a breakdown in relations among its members. (Within 18 months the RADA initiative had failed. The services of their Managing Director were dispensed with and RADA reverted to a two-tiered model in which administration and artistic direction were again separated.)

It is against this background that Lynne Williams was recruited to the new position of Director and Chief Executive. However, before we venture there, I want to consider the intellectual and educational underpinnings of arts training in Australia.

2

Arts training in Australia

Compared with some of the other art forms in Australia, theatre training has received scant attention from policy makers, either in government or the bureaucracy. Two recent reports, one on the craft sector (the Myer Report) and the other on Indigenous art, along with the Australia Council's evaluation of the *Visual Arts and Craft Strategy 2004–2009*, have contained significant recommendations about supporting and upgrading levels of teaching in the visual arts and crafts sector.[13] The Myer Report was particularly strong in relation to funding for short-to-medium-term professional development of arts and crafts centre staff, as well as for formal teaching staff.

By contrast, when it comes to the performing arts and filmmaking, almost no attention has been paid to questions of fundamental education and training. Successive national governments have invested large sums in support of both of these industries but there has never been an independent or parliamentary inquiry into arts training as such. There are programs and support networks to help theatre practitioners establish performing arts companies and gain funding but almost no advice on what constitutes proper student training.

This lack of attention to fundamental questions of basic theatre training pervades even the submissions made by NIDA and other training institutions to the ongoing National Cultural Policy review.[14] Although the NIDA submission touches upon the skills required by art/theatre teachers in schools (in reference to the forthcoming national curriculum), a close reading reveals little attempt to define what constitutes good or bad practice in theatre training or how the former might be encouraged. Nicky McWilliam focussed upon the plight of the fine arts, observing:

> It is possible to complete a graduate and even postgraduate degree in fine art, visual art, arts administration or arts

11

*theory at an Australian university without acquiring
even the most basic knowledge about Australian art or
art history;*

and lamented the continuation of a dysfunctional
cultural cringe trumpeting the superiority of European-
American art over Australian'.[15] Reviewing the creative
arts in Australia, Terry Cutler noted:

*There is no national approach to essential training for
these industries, nor capacity to train to an appropriate
level all the talented students seeking to participate in the
creative arts.*[16]

This applies equally to theatre training so that in
the absence of any attempt at objective measurement
it depends upon the skills of the individual teacher
or practitioner. Those who are charged with the
responsibility to educate our doctors, nurses,
teachers, engineers must reach set standards to be
judged qualified. They may also need to be 'certified'
and are increasingly required to be 'refreshed'. No
such strictures need apply to those who teach our
performing artists. (However, I acknowledge that
Lynne Williams initially undertook a benchmarking
of NIDA *courses* against overseas institutions which
resulted in a generally favourable assessment.)[17]

So long as this is the case, the artistic director of any
training institution bears an enormous responsibility
to ensure that the best teachers are chosen and the
curriculum is of the highest level, having regard
to prevailing international and local professional
standards and requirements. That is the minimum
requirement for an artistic director in the professional
performing arts.

3

The Director and
Chief Executive

The appointment in 2008 of Lynne Williams to the position as Director and Chief Executive of NIDA is one of the defining moments in the school's history. The appointment, and her subsequent tenure, split the then Board, and has led to the departure (in almost all cases in unhappy or hostile circumstances) of almost all the senior artistic staff.

It was during Aubrey Mellor's tenure as Director that cracks had begun to appear. Butcher's impending retirement had been badly handled (Board member Bruce Cutler admitted, 'We f...ed up'[18]) and Malcolm Long was brought in as Chair to replace Jillian Broadbent. During 2007 it became apparent that relations between Mellor and the Board had also deteriorated. Mellor was placed on a series of one-year renewable contracts. When news of his impending departure was leaked it provoked representations to Chairman Long in support of Mellor's reappointment. On 27 February 2008 Long received a letter signed by Neil Armfield (Artistic Director, Company B) on behalf of most of the leading lights of Australian theatre. Long's reply attached a copy of a statement issued on 5 December 2007 in which he had announced a Board decision to restructure the executive management of

NIDA. What he wrote is critical for an understanding of subsequent events:

> *The Board decided that a new position of Director of NIDA will be created, clearly designated as chief executive officer, responsible for the education and training of NIDA students, the development of NIDA's artistic and educational vision, the strategic management of NIDA, the leadership of staff and the implementation and communications of NIDA's mission internally, to the industry and the community at large.[…] The board also decided that the important position of General Manager would be retained; responsible to the new Director for managing the financial, technical and administrative services of NIDA, including its policy development, regulatory obligations and commercial activities, and to assist the Director in the overall leadership of the institute.*[19]

At this point the roles of director and general manager were seen being filled by two people. In an interview a few days later he was reported as saying that it was '*highly likely*' that the new head would have a theatre background:

> *We are looking for a person with strong performance, theatrical and media experience, and credibility in that area, but who can also play the wider role of bringing all the aspects of keeping an institution like NIDA together and moving forward.*[20]

In briefings to staff, Long assured them the new Director would be '*a leading member of the profession*' and that a General Manager would be appointed to assist.

The Chair was thus clearly on record as making two promises: that the new Director would be a (leading) theatre-person and that NIDA would also have a General Manager. The fact that neither of these things came to pass is now a matter of record. Indeed, after Williams' appointment and despite the promises, it was Long who moved to amend the NIDA Constitution to abolish the position of General Manager.

The search for a new Director was undertaken in the first instance by Julie Steiner of Braithwaite Steiner Pretty Global Search. The Key Responsibilities listed in the *Information for Candidates* pack included (inter alia) to:

- provide leadership and a strong artistic and educational vision for NIDA
- supervise the NIDA Teaching program and the NIDA Play Production program
- appoint teaching staff and select students for full-time courses.

This clearly implied that the Director would have a strong artistic and teaching/educational background; skills to supervise play productions and the knowledge/experience to audition and select students for all NIDA courses.

There was a strong field of candidates. On 15 March 2008 Valerie Lawson, writing in the *Sydney Morning Herald*, revealed that there were five internal applicants (including Mellor reapplying for his own position).[21] She noted that the shortlist of considered candidates included NIDA Deputy Director Peter Cooke[22] and internationally renowned theatre director and teacher Gale Edwards; and went on to report (correctly) that the choice made by the Board was for an 'outside candidate, an Australian who has been working overseas'; that 'the Board was not unanimous in its choice' and that the preferred candidate was strongly supported by Long and Board members Pamela Rabe and Tom Jeffrey. Williams was appointed on 15 April 2008.

Williams had been a primary school teacher 1968–75, and from 1977–82 lectured in education and the performing arts at the University of Wollongong with an emphasis on voice training.[23] Her initial training was at the Conservatorium of Music, a very different model from that used for actors. In 1985 she moved to the United Kingdom and settled there until her return for interviews for the NIDA position. In the UK she held administrative positions in a variety of arts organisations, undertook the promotion and organisation of arts touring products in the east of England, was CEO of Cardiff's unsuccessful bid to be European City of Culture (2008) and held a variety of short-term contracts in developing the cultural aspect of London's 2012 Olympics bid.

Her CV makes it clear that Williams has never directed a significant theatre performance; taught acting students; supervised theatre training or auditioned students for placement in a training institution or ever earned a living in the professional theatre. Indeed, during a conversation with myself and others, we put the question: how would she respond to finding out a week before opening that a major student production was in danger of not being up to standard? What would she do about it? She replied, not that she would appoint another director or rescue it herself, but that she would 'cancel' it. That may be a fair enough response in a commercial environment, but hardly fair on the students. None of her positions has involved providing a 'strong artistic or educational vision', nor sustaining or improving standards of artistic excellence. Her great skills are in administration and co-ordination. Nor has she been responsible for the development of curricula or teaching methods in a vocational theatre school. For the previous twenty years she had lived outside Australia. How this measured up against the promises of a new Director as a 'leading member of the profession' or a person with a 'strong performance or theatrical experience' is questionable in light of those Directors with whom NIDA's might be compared: Sandra Levy (AFTRS), Julie Warn (WAAPA), Su Baker (VCA), Karl Kramer (NSW Conservatorium of Music), Marilyn Rowe (Australian Ballet School), Kim Walker (NAISDA), Sarah Miller (University of Wollongong Drama School), Dean Carey (Actors' Centre), Andrew Schultz (UNSW School of Arts and Media), Pam Creed (National Institute of Circus Arts).

Interestingly, Williams herself appeared to believe at this time that a general manager would be appointed. She stated in writing her determination to see this happen, and to develop a 'strategy to attract and retain high calibre teaching staff'.She also committed to improving NIDA's external relationships and to establish a Contemporary Practice Research Unit within the first two years of her appointment.[24]

Clearly the key role of the Director of NIDA must be to develop and articulate the educational and artistic vision for the School in regard to which Lynne Williams referred me to the Australian Universities Quality Agency (AUQA) report of 2010 and her reports in each of the NIDA *Annual Reports*. I found the AUQA report instructive. Dealing with the effectiveness in teaching, learning and other core functions it observes:

NIDA has some established teaching and learning approaches and frameworks in place, but these need to be rethought to better reflect the current context. The challenge for NIDA is to consider the practice of teaching and learning within a creative context, achieving a balance between industry professional practice and an academic approach to teaching and learning.

The report queried the 'efficiency' of those courses at NIDA with only minimal enrolments noting:

At present NIDA is not providing a conceptual space for teachers to come together and discuss pedagogy [...] currently NIDA is unable to define the characteristics that are being cultivated in students through the curriculum.[25]

I have seen few, if any, responses to these criticisms but many in the industry would be alarmed at any move to shift the balance from 'professional practice' to 'an academic' approach to teaching when those same industry professionals were already recorded in the AUQA report as expressing concerns about the level of current students' preparedness to enter the profession on graduation. Equally, I see inherent difficulty when a Director has no immediate professional experience as a pedagogue in leading a process for creating the 'conceptual space' referred to in the report.

Turning to the Director's Report in NIDA's *Annual Reports*,[26] the first of these (2008) refers to the need for NIDA graduates to be

equipped for an environment in which arts and technology are converging. Film, television, animation, events, computer games and digital media forms are increasingly offering significant employment opportunities to graduates of all courses.

Nothing is said, however, of what changes NIDA would make to accommodate these new realities. Instead, the largest section of the report announces that 'NIDA's vision for the future is best summed up in the desire to build our postgraduate program into an International Centre for Contemporary Performance Practice' (CCPP) the virtues of which are extolled at length. Feasibility studies and funding applications apart, there is no sign yet of such a Centre nor any prospect of there being one. Nothing in the 2008 report deals with any sense of artistic or educational vision or any commitment to positive action towards enhancing artistic or educational outcomes.

The 2009 Report refers again to the 'rapidly evolving needs of the global arts and entertainment industry' and the need to offer 'higher education courses which will nurture future leaders and agents of change and ensure the creativity and innovation that are central to the future of the industry'. This is to be done primarily through the CCPP.

The 2010 Report noted:

> *we took another step closer to achieving our visions for a Centre for Contemporary Performance Practice [through which] we want to ensure that Australians are at the forefront of research into a broad range of new and emerging performance contexts and have entrepreneurial skills to turn innovative ideas into viable initiatives.*

Finally in 2011: 'NIDA needs to continue to transform as an institution and strive to become a centre for dynamic thought-leadership and a catalyst for change within the industry.' Plans are announced for a new course entitled 'Cultural Leadership' aimed at developing 'the movers and shakers who will help create an Australia that understands and values culture'. This course would be offered 'within our proposed Centre for Contemporary Performance Practice'.

Behind the jargon ('thought leadership', 'movers and shakers', 'catalyst for change') there is nothing in the Director's reports which would allow any appreciation that a genuine sense of vision in terms of educational or artistic leadership is present in NIDA, or that steps, other than consultants' reports and feasibility studies, have been taken towards shaping the intellectual base of the CCPP. Equally, there is a complete absence of any significant mention of Indigenous Australia or awareness of what is happening in Asia or our region. The idea that NIDA might have a pivotal role to play in the 'soft diplomacy' now practised by sophisticated nations and cultural institutions appears to have passed without notice.

'Where there is no vision, the people perish', said the prophet.[27] Williams has had success in securing some increased commercial sponsorship, promoting more film and television training, revising, revamping and introducing some new courses;[28] and establishing 'creative transformation' as the school's new mantra. Time will judge whether on these foundations her stewardship will be seen as having taken NIDA to new and greater heights.

4

Management
of Staff

As Tolstoy observed, each unhappy family is unhappy in its own way. Nothing could be more illustrative of the transition from 'old' to 'new' at NIDA than the collapse of the 'family' atmosphere which had characterised the place for the better part of four decades.

Managing staff at NIDA has never been a simple undertaking—artistic temperaments are never easy to manage, and throughout its history NIDA has been blessed with a superabundance of these. It would be foolish, and indeed inaccurate, to say that there were never personality clashes, tensions or significant disagreements among staff members in its history. The more serious disagreements have tended to involve problems with students and occasionally with NIDA Board members but staff and senior management have nevertheless regarded themselves as 'family' and there has been a high level of out-of-school socialisation among staff at all levels and between teaching and administrative staff.

New NIDA has no time for such niceties and the past four years are littered with the remnants of shattered members of staff, collegiality sacrificed on the altar of corporatism. Some of the longest serving, most dedicated and talented members of staff were summarily marched off the premises and told they were no longer of any use to the school. Staff with over twenty years' service left, refusing due recognition of their departure.

This lack of generosity to those who resigned, or were pushed out, for their failure to adapt to the new paradigm, was clearly illustrated when Elizabeth Butcher left in 2008. Her departure was recorded in that year's *Annual Report* by a mere fourteen words in the Chairman's Report and the addition of her name to the names of five other departing staff in the Director's Report. No photo of Butcher was included and no attempt was made to recognise her *forty years* of incomparable service.

Similarly in the 2011 *Annual Report* the departure of nine staff members with a collective service of over a century was only briefly recognised, with no acknowledgement of the significance of their contribution. Informal familial courtesies that had been practised by Butcher over many years have also been discarded.

Since 2008 the attrition of staff of the Clark/ Butcher era has been formidable. Gone are not only Elizabeth Butcher (General Manager), but Peter Cooke (Deputy Director and Head of Design), Amanda Morris (Head of Open Program), Barbara Warren (Head of Corporate Performance), Bill Pepper (Head of Voice Studies), Julia Cotton (Head of Movement Studies), Tony Knight (Head of Acting), Kevin Jackson (senior Acting Teacher), Avigail Herman (Music Theatre teacher), Christine Roberts (Senior Librarian), Betty Williams (Senior Voice teacher), Kathryn Adler (Archive Curator) and Lyn Pierse (Improvisation teacher). All these practitioners left in circumstances of disagreement. For example Hermann's departure coincided with Williams' sudden axing of the Music Theatre course—one of the most successful of NIDA's offerings—and a decision to take up to eight 'music theatre' type students into each first year class of 25 or 26 students.

In addition there were departures by Tim Patston (Head of Music), Antoinette Blaxland (Acting Teacher), Russell Mitchell (Technical Director), Shaun Luttrell (Senior Accountant) and Susie Osborn (Archive Curator). Craig Meagher, the Marketing Manager recruited by Williams to turn around NIDA's financial fortunes, left after barely a year and four other members of the marketing staff departed, one after only two weeks. At the time of writing, another Williams' appointee, Jane Brodie (Head of Playwriting), has submitted her resignation. Of the 76 staff members listed on Williams' arrival only 21 remained by 2012 and of the nine core teaching staff (Acting/Design/Direction) only two.[29]

It is natural, indeed necessary, that there be a regular turnover of staff in any dynamic organisation. However, a skilful management would ensure that this process of change and renewal was not accompanied by tears and lingering hostility. The majority of those on this list have had no qualms about expressing to me their resentment at what they saw as a coherent and determined policy to remove all vestiges of the previous era at NIDA.

It is worth looking at some of those departures in detail to gain a better understanding of just how things have changed.[30]

Christine Roberts started in the NIDA Library in 1980 and by 2009 had built it into an outstanding performing arts library and resource. She was also by then one of the most universally loved members of staff, especially by the students who found in her a guide and mentor.

The trouble began when on arrival at NIDA, Williams, with no familiarity with NIDA's library services, determined on a 'review'. An external review made a series of recommendations, which focussed on stretching the professional staff over longer hours or more shifts, to which was added a proposal to reduce the space and the range of books to provide for 'tutorial rooms'. Over Roberts' objection to the loss of space and what she believed was a lack of professional understanding of NIDA's library requirements management adopted the review's findings. She noted at the time that, while many recommendations were in line with what she herself had been advocating, other parts contained 'mistakes and misconceptions'.[31]

The plan to cut the physical space in the library was presented to Roberts on 10 September by three members of management and without consultation. It went much further than the addition of extra study rooms to which she had already agreed. So, on 17 September, after 29 years' service, Roberts decided that she was not prepared to watch the Library being devalued and tendered her resignation. In an email to all staff she stated:

> *There are many changes mooted and underway, some of which, in my opinion and experience, will result in a serious loss of service to the NIDA students and staff. I have no desire to witness and facilitate the deterioration of the principles on which this library's excellence is based.*

While this might be seen as simply a disagreement in principle between a specialist and administration, what is more significant is the conclusion of Roberts' email:

> *I choose not to work in an environment in which I feel intimidated and bullied, and in which my qualifications, ability and experience are not respected.*

This is serious criticism, but more to the point it is a public statement that a senior member of NIDA staff believed herself subject to bullying and intimidation. Recent changes in workplace laws and practices make it clear that allegations of bullying are matters which need to be addressed. In a response to staff Williams wrote simply: 'I do not accept Christine's comment that there has been an environment of intimidation or bullying around the recent discussions.' Management made no attempt to persuade Roberts to reconsider her position, nor did the Board investigate her serious allegations. She left, declining Williams' offer of a farewell 'celebration' and took up a position in the library of the Australian Film Television and Radio School.

Bill Pepper is one of Australia's pre-eminent voice teachers and coaches, a perfect gentleman and another long-serving NIDA staff member (1981–6, 1995–2010). One day he and two other staff members were walking through the NIDA car park when he noticed a tray of rat poison. On impulse he removed the label and affixed it (without damage) to the side window of Williams' car, parked adjacent. When the action and its implications were discovered, Pepper immediately admitted to the misdemeanour and awaited punishment. What he did not expect was a visit from the Maroubra Police, to investigate. When the police took no action a firm of private investigators was called in from Canberra. Pepper was formally reprimanded by the Chair and departed quietly. His departure was not recorded in the subsequent *Annual Report*.

Kevin Jackson as Senior Acting Teacher was one of the intellectual powerhouses of NIDA. His knowledge of plays, especially new Australian work, was exceptional. Jackson had taught at NIDA for 17 years and on 30 December 2011 his contract for a three-year term with two-year extension was due for renewal. With the departure of Tony Knight (see Chapter 5) Jackson was effectively holding the fort for the Acting course while a new Head was sought. He was an applicant for this position and, according to the students, their preferred candidate. But at management level respect for his experience appeared negligible. The candidate appointed as Interim Head of Acting was the Head of Music. Staff and students were alarmed, and not without reason. It became clear that Jackson would be offered neither the Head of Acting nor the two-year extension, but one year only. This was unacceptable to him: his entitlement was for two and there were no performance issues to justify a reduction.

Jackson had not made things easier for himself by his repeated clashes with Williams, whom he regarded as unqualified. He had been a vocal supporter of Christine Roberts and taken a leading role in opposing her departure. He was subsequently reprimanded for circulating an article from the *My Career* section of the *Sydney Morning Herald* entitled 'Mean Girls' which had as its subheading 'There are some nasty women at work and they're targeting other females'. Perhaps a little close to the bone.

NIDA's Christmas Party that year was held on 9 December and its venue the old White House on the campus of UNSW. To those familiar with NIDA's history this was the building in which NIDA was first established. This would probably not have been known to some of the newer members of NIDA staff, so Jackson decided to alert them. In an email to all staff, dated 8 December, he wrote:

> *The delightful irony, for me, of our Christmas Party VENUE is that it is a standing survivor, a relic, from what has been known, of late, as 'Old NIDA'. It was, in days of yore, the Staff and Administrative building. It has witnessed many a NIDA Party. That we are celebrating, perhaps, dancing, on its boards (Grave!), within its white, sepulchral walls, only history (fact) would dare write. [...] Thought I should, could, share, the irony. Happy Holidays, Kevin*

The same day he received a formal letter from NIDA management:

> *I refer to your email to all staff and external parties regarding the venue for the Christmas party, which was inappropriate and not in accordance with the NIDA Code of Conduct [...] I am issuing you with a formal direction not to return to NIDA for the duration of your employment, which concludes on 30 December 2011. In my absence on leave [...] you can contact [...] regarding having access to your office to remove any personal items and return NIDA property.*

Jackson took his troubles to the National Tertiary Education Union. Other NIDA staff followed. The Union's efforts secured him his ten-year long-service leave entitlement in August 2011, not February 2012, as notified, which would have compelled him to sign the one-year contract to which he had objected. Jackson's anathematisation was complete enough for another teacher to be flown from Melbourne to undertake the Chekhov immersion program, which had been Jackson's special province and which he had offered to continue teaching on a part-time basis.

The Head of Corporate Performance, who prefers not to be named here, was one of the stars of the fundraising pantheon at NIDA. She arrived in February 1996 to take over as Head of the Open Program during a period in which Amanda Morris was involved in the production of NIDA's BAFTA-winning CD *Stagestruck*. In 2003 she moved across to head the Corporate Program which, between 2003 and 2010 grew from a revenue base of $200,000 to in excess of $2million. At no stage was her performance criticised; indeed, she claimed the Director had discussed her work with her no more than twice between 2008 and 2010. Nevertheless, without consultation, Williams appointed a 'supremo' to oversee the Open, Corporate, Development and Marketing departments—Craig Meagher. He had a background in sports marketing and had worked at the Sydney Cricket and Sports Ground Trust. He was gone within the year but left a legacy of 'stretch budgets' that imposed unfair stress on already hardworking and productive staff. When the Head objected, she too was first sidelined and then informed, by yet another external consultant, that the Board had determined she was 'too expensive' and her services were no longer required. She was told to leave the premises immediately and her personal effects would be forwarded to her. She refused to leave in that fashion and returned to her office to pack, under the supervision of the Human Resources staff. Pressure was applied for her to sign documents relating to her termination payments, which she refused to do in the absence of professional advice. The matter went before Fair Work Australia but remains unresolved. Entitlements and redundancy payments remain unpaid.

One could multiply such instances:

Lyn Pierse was a casual employee but the finest improvisation teacher in the country, with 22 years' service at NIDA and authorship of the definitive training manual on the subject.[32] It was only on the resumption of first term 2012 that she learned that her services were no longer required and was given a small payout.

Amanda Morris, one of only two PhDs at NIDA, creator of the Open Program, producer of the interactive CD *Stagestruck*, left after being told peremptorily that 'there was no future for her at NIDA'. Recognition of her BAFTA Award was omitted from the brief issued for recruitment of the Head of Acting whereas those for Cate Blanchett and Baz Luhrmann were highlighted.

Kathryn Adler found her position in the Archives abolished without adequate consultation. The matter ended in the Industrial Relations Commission but was eventually discontinued when Adler could no longer pay her legal fees.

As a matter of policy it appears that NIDA's non-administrative staff—nearly all of them in teaching—are now to be offered only three-year contracts with a possible two-year extension; and that no contract will be available beyond five years. This will preclude there developing a teaching staff with the length of service and stability that has been so essential to NIDA's artistic and educational development. I cannot emphasise how retrograde I regard this step and how much I fear it will be the death knell of quality teaching at NIDA. Great teachers do not necessarily reach their peak in any one institution in just a few short years, they grow into those roles over time. To me this is a painful reminder of Lynne Williams' failure to understand what acting teaching is about.

It also means that under current employment provisions staff can no longer claim to be permanent employees. This stricture does not apply to administrative staff, so for the first time in NIDA's history the staff has two classes—those who have tenure and those who can serve for only five years—just about enough time to dissuade any professional from seeing teaching as a promising alternative career. Williams has recently had her own three-year contract extended, apparently for three years.

5

Acting wars

If a tree is known by its fruit, then NIDA is known by the outstanding quality of its graduates, in particular the actors—its 'primary business'.[33] To look at the list of NIDA Acting graduates is to see the bedrock upon which Australian theatre, film and television has been grounded for the last several decades: Colin Friels, Judy Davis, Mel Gibson, Steve Bisley, John Howard, Hugo Weaving, Baz Luhrmann, Richard Roxburgh, Jacqueline McKenzie, Miranda Otto, Cate Blanchett, Helen Dallimore, Susie Porter, Sam Worthington, Toby Schmitz, Yael Stone, Eamon Farren, Hugh Sheridan, Jessica Marais, Ryan Corrs, Meyne Wyatt...

The Acting course at NIDA has had a solid underpinning in theory as well as in the practice of 'learning by doing'. It has also sought to support a uniquely Australian approach and to develop a uniquely Australian style.[34] (It went so far as to take steps to prevent an American institution from offering what it advertised as 'the NIDA method' of teaching.) This was based on an approach which focussed on the trilogy of *talent* (realised through a rigorous audition process), *technique* (taught across all disciplines) and *temperament* (the encouragement of what David Malouf's 1998 Boyer Lectures described as 'a spirit of play').[35] Intellectually it harks back to both Stanislavski and, perhaps more significantly, the work of Michel Saint-Denis.[36] It draws on English tradition and American practice of theatre training but adds a uniquely Australian dimension, especially in relation to encouraging the physicality of actors and that one thing that so identifies an Australian performing artist: an understanding of the use of space.[37]

Pedagogically, following Saint-Denis, NIDA treated students as if they were diamonds. In First Year, the accretions of bad habits were gradually chipped away; in Second Year the stone was cut and facetted; and in Third Year it was polished.[38] First Year was all about technique, with an introduction to naturalism (generally Chekhov) and at the end of the year students were placed in their first full productions. Second Year traditionally saw them performing a Shakespeare and a comedy while in Third Year there would be productions of Australian or international works or a musical, and preparation for their graduate showcase pieces. This model was developed by a series of Heads of Acting, including John Bell, George Whaley, Nick Enright, Kevin Jackson, Aubrey Mellor, Dean Carey, Tony Taylor and Tony Knight.

Within a few months of her arrival at NIDA, the Acting course became a battleground between Williams and the Acting staff, supported by a certain element of the Board. Very early in her tenure Williams had reported to the Board that she thought the Acting department 'dysfunctional' and its teaching methods 'old fashioned'.

At a Planning Day in July 2009, I presented a lengthy paper arguing that the centrality of the Acting course at NIDA was being diminished, that the department was being denied resources, that plays and external directors were being chosen without sufficient consultation with the Acting staff, and that students were being pushed into public performances too early. The then Head of Acting, Tony Knight, finding his response inhibited, offered to put his views in writing. Chairman Long then terminated debate, promised to list the matter for later discussion with Knight's paper to hand, and assured people it would be circulated. In the event, the paper (dated 14 August) was suppressed and the matter never raised again. Subsequently the Director gave a scathing assessment of the Acting department and some of its teachers and proposed a complete overhaul.

First the Director instructed the Acting department to undertake a complete self-review of its courses, which it did in May 2010. This was followed by a review under the aegis of the Board of Studies, with specific input from Board member Pamela Rabe and an external review conducted by Professor Margareta Schuler benchmarking against Berlin's Ernst Busch School. A selective and secret survey was also conducted, but whatever their outcomes they were never made available to the Acting department and Tony Knight was denied access.

Knight, followed by senior Acting teacher Kevin Jackson, was soon on his way out. Knight and Jackson's effective removal, along with the departure of Julia Cotton in Movement, now left the way open for a radical overhaul of the Acting course. A new Head of Acting had to be recruited.

6

Jeff Janisheski: The Nice Man Cometh

Head of Acting at NIDA is a prize to which many artists at the top of their experience aspire and the names of those who applied were no secret to the profession. Suffice to say that in 2009 the list included some of Australia's most distinguished teachers and actors and Australians from a variety of cultural backgrounds with great experience in Australian theatre.

Overwhelmingly within the School, the student body and the profession there was a keen desire for this new leader to be an Australian, to be familiar with Australian theatre history and practice, pedagogy and writing, culture and contemporary debate, and above all with aspects of Australia's Indigenous and multicultural national conversation. None of this was reflected in the brief for candidates prepared by Braithwaite Steiner Pretty, which in its selection criteria section did not mention the words 'Australia' or 'Australian' once. The Director also made it clear in comments widely reported within the profession that she did not regard any Australian applicant as qualified for the position.

The new Head of Acting, appointed in November 2011, was an American.

Jeff Janisheski was then head of the National Theatre Institute (NTI) at the Eugene O'Neill Theatre Centre where he taught a one-semester 'fourteen week study-away program […] offered twice a year'. Of the fourteen weeks, two weeks were spent at academies abroad. The Acting course is described as having 'classes which concentrate on improving your craft as an actor and on strengthening your intelligence and imagination as an artist.'[39]

I am in no way questioning Janisheski's experience as an acting teacher. The question that arises is: how well can a person who has been teaching fourteen-week courses design and manage a curriculum across a three-year, and potentially four-year, degree course? Further, how will his limited knowledge of both the

NIDA's traditions and methods and the recent history of Australian theatre performance, writing, cultural debate and Indigenous/multicultural conversation affect his capacity to respond to the needs of the profession?

The NTI was initiated at the O'Neill in 1970, and is a small part of the main School. NIDA has been somewhat disingenuous in its description of this relationship. In the 2011 edition of *NIDA News*, Janisheski is described as 'an Artistic Director at the acclaimed Eugene O'Neill Theatre Centre';[40] and the press release announcing his appointment refers to Broadway productions developed at the O'Neill but unrelated to any activities of the NTI.[41]

From the decision taken so far (he arrived in January) it is now clear that Janisheski plans to turn the old NIDA Acting course paradigm on its head.[42] Although the final version of his new three-year curriculum has yet to be published, it is understood that he proposes to run a first-year two-stream course of scene work based on the twin pillars of realism/ naturalism (Chekhov/O'Neill/Miller) on the one hand and heightened language awareness (Greeks/ Shakespeare/Moliere) on the other. This raises the question, of students' maturity to take on the Greeks in their first year and then the possibility of students graduating from NIDA without ever having performed in a full Shakespeare production.[43] I raise no objection to regular revisions of courses, but to do so, so soon after arrival, is bound to raise a degree of apprehension.

One immediate innovation appears to be a radical rethinking of the audition process for entry to NIDA. In previous years all auditionees have been required to present two pieces, one from Shakespeare and one from a contemporary Australian play. This gave assessors the opportunity to judge a candidate's capacity to handle heightened language and their comfort with contemporary language and ideas. It is understood (subject to correction) that the 2012 auditions will require the presentation of only one piece of the candidate's own choice.

Jeff Janisheski has my sympathy; he is very much alone. However, it is too early yet to comment on what are only reported changes; my fears may yet prove groundless.

7

Indigenous Australia and the Asian environment

The last few years have seen a wonderful burgeoning of both interest and activity in the exposure of white Australia to the world's oldest living culture, especially its art. A new group of Indigenous theatre makers—playwrights, directors, dancers, actors, musicians—has emerged bringing a unique perspective to the ongoing debate about what it means to be Australian.[44] Similarly, as our political engagement with Asia, and our redefined role as a leading nation of the South-west Pacific, has forced us to face up to our new international responsibilities, an increasing number of Australian artists have recognised the need for cultural engagement with Asia. The principles of 'soft-diplomacy' are increasingly being seen as vital to our strategic and economic wellbeing.[45] Serious engagement with both Indigenous Australia and with Asia is something which the new NIDA has, with deliberation, sought to evade.

The Director's choice of Artists in Residence so far has managed to include a Russian, two Germans, a Frenchman, an American and an associate from London. Her choice of plays has not included anything outside the Australian (white)/European/American: repertoire. Almost none of the designs of any NIDA production has reflected an Indigenous or Asian aesthetic. The incorporation of history of Asian theatre into the appropriate academic part of the course has been minimal.

When Dr Ken Henry (conducting a review for the Federal Government on 'The Asian Century') remarks that 'educational institutions [...] would also be called on to adopt and apply the new mindset of the Asian century', this apparently fails to resound with anyone in the NIDA leadership.[46] Design students head off regularly to the Prague Quadrennial (properly recognised as a leading forum for participation) but never to the Peking Opera or any of the great venues in India.

As the Australian population changes, so do the demographics of NIDA's students. An increasing number of Indigenous and Asian students enter the courses, but there is no attempt to bring with them plays about dispossession, reconciliation, migration, or refugees which might reflect their backgrounds, community or cultural identities.

It was not always so. Elizabeth Butcher served on the Board of NAISDA. Peter Cooke taught each year in India, and in Tonga, Vietnam and the Philippines; and his designs reflected this. John Clark and Aubrey Mellor both undertook extensive teaching in China and Singapore and Mellor mounted Indigenous plays when Director of the Malthouse.[47] To date, the best NIDA has managed in its new incarnation has been to invite Lee Lewis, a NIDA graduate who has been actively engaged with Indigenous and non-Caucasian actors, to work there occasionally. In 2012 the Indigenous actor and filmmaker Wayne Blair was invited to join the Board following election by members but resigned almost immediately due to pressure of other commitments. He was replaced by Ralph Myers, the busy Artistic Director of Belvoir Street Theatre. Thus the NIDA Board still has no Indigenous representation, nor indeed is there any among the senior staff.

Although the NIDA Board has no responsibility for the selection of students, staff (other than the CEO) or plays, it does have responsibility under NIDA's Constitution to set strategic policy and monitor educational and artistic performance.

8

External relations

One of the key tasks for any Director of NIDA is to build and develop external contacts and important relationships.

NIDA's principal funder is the Australian Government, and Williams inherited a solid foundation of mutual respect from her predecessors. Federal Ministers get a great buzz from visiting and funding NIDA, given that it occupies a spectacular Commonwealth-owned building, and its base funding has never been seriously at risk. However, funding for special projects, such as Elizabeth Butcher had from the Centenary of Federation Fund for the Stage 2 development of NIDA, has not been forthcoming since her departure. NIDA has been provided with some small enhancement of its funding, most of which has gone towards required increases in salaries for existing staff.

On the other hand, relations with one of NIDA's most generous private supporters, the Seaborn, Broughton and Walford Foundation (SBWF), have entered more stormy waters. The Foundation was established by the late Dr Rodney Seaborn (1912–2008), a noted philanthropist and a man with a particular devotion to NIDA, nurtured by Butcher. Since Williams's arrival there have been differences with the SBWF. The first of these was the SBWF's eviction from a room in the NIDA building which served as Dr Seaborn's office. Then came a difference over the resourcing of the

SBW Theatre Archives (which, co-mingled with those of NIDA constituted one of the best theatre archives in Australia). The SBW archives moved out to premises of their own, at considerable cost and the collection was split. Since then the SBWF has also expressed concern over the nature and quality of the new Artists in Residence program to which SBW money has been applied. Not all NIDA's recent requests for funding have been supported.

Another disaffected donor is the Sydney entertainment personality Mike Walsh, who became friends with Elizabeth Butcher in 1996 when she was Chair of the Sydney Opera House Trust. An outcome was that he announced his intention to recognise NIDA in his will and agreed to fund a series of scholarships to assist NIDA graduates in the further development of their careers. These grants were then worth up to $30,000. After Butcher's departure the relationship between Walsh and NIDA deteriorated, and in 2011 he decided that VCA and WAAPA graduates would also be eligible. In that year a NIDA graduate won only one of the four major (now $50,000) grants on offer.

In similar vein another of NIDA's faithful donors effectively withdrew from direct support as a result of Williams's appointment, deeming her to be unqualified, and in protest at her intervention in the plans to celebrate NIDA's fiftieth anniversary. He told *Sydney Morning Herald* writer Bryce Hallett that under Williams, planned initiatives to mark NIDA's fiftieth anniversary had been shelved, opportunities lost and no lasting benefits achieved: 'There was an almost complete failure to extract any significant advantage out of the NIDA fiftieth anniversary celebrations with no significant increase in funding, scholarships or other lasting benefits.'[48] I am also aware of at least four people who have, as a result of NIDA's regime change, written the school out of their wills—in some cases the sums in question were substantial.

NIDA has also failed to engage in any of the debates about the future of theatre in Sydney or the wider discussion of performance education. NIDA representatives do not attend the meetings of the developing Sydney Theatre Network and there was no mention of NIDA in the significant two-part analysis of performance education in *Real Time* magazine.[49]

On the other hand, in 2010 Williams and Long achieved a major new commercial sponsorship from the Seven Television Network to provide some $1 million over five years, which was used primarily to upgrade the in-house television training facilities at NIDA. These will also be used by Seven's own people to do 'master classes'. NIDA has a long history of working with television stations going back to the days when representatives of both the ABC and SBS sat on the NIDA Board and students went for regular training at the old ABC studios. However, for many years students have sought access to more and better facilities to train in acting-for-the-camera and these improvements are welcome.

Needless to say there will always be questions of how a public education institution manages its relationship with external funding providers in a fiercely competitive marketplace, but the benefit to NIDA students of the in-house facility is undoubted.[50] The Seven sponsorship featured as a major element in the brief prepared, and widely circulated, for the Head of Acting recruitment exercise.

9

Students

NIDA is supposed to be all about its students but it is they who have suffered from the events of the last few years.

In 2011, a group of Year 2 Acting students conducted an unprecedented on-line survey among students in their Acting course. More than 50 of the approximately 70 students responded. Questions were general issues related to the course, and more specific assessments of individual teachers, the leadership of NIDA, the role of the Board and the way in which they were treated personally.[51] Evaluation of the principal teachers was on the basis of being asked: 'Do you think that the teachers are fulfilling their role to the degree that you would expect from a National institute?' Only the six senior teachers heading each course were assessed. Results ranged from a positive assessment of four of them—between 86% and 98%—and of the remaining two one was rated positively by 46% (with 32% negative and 22% undecided) and the other by only 30% (44% negative and 26% undecided). Two of the top four have since departed.

To the question: 'Are you happy with the current state of the Acting Course?', 64% responded 'no' and one teacher bore most opprobrium for this. To the question: 'Do you have confidence in the current leadership of NIDA?' 64% responded negatively. Asked if they had confidence in the current administrative procedures for dealing with grievances, 76% said 'no' and when asked about the maintenance of their privacy in grievance or assessment proceedings, this negative response hit 84%. When asked if they thought that the Board of Directors was aware of what was happening at a student level, the negative response was 82%. (For many years a student representative had sat, by invitation, on the NIDA Board, a practice now discontinued.) Asked if they thought that the roles of Artistic Director and CEO should be kept separate, this was favoured by 90%. Most ominously, when asked the question: 'Are you worried about the reputation of NIDA declining in the professional community?' the response was 84% yes, 12% no and 4% undecided. The students sent a copy of this survey to senior figures in management, and to various members of the NIDA Board and Board of Studies. Not one person responded.

A separate communication to Lynne Williams from the Acting students offering support for Kevin Jackson and asking for his consideration as the new Head of Acting, was dismissed with the advice that 'you must now trust that the recruitment of the new Head of Acting will be handled skilfully by the experts' and that 'it is now time for you to concentrate on your own work'.

Above all, Acting students complained about the quality of the Movement course. This was, until 2010, one of the great achievements of NIDA, pioneered by the legendary Keith Bain.[52] Bain joined NIDA on a part-time basis in 1965 and became full-time in 1977. The first group of students for his full-time course included Judy Davis, Steve Bisley and Mel Gibson. He designed first the undergraduate and then the postgraduate Movement courses through which he profoundly influenced generations of Australian actors. His story was the inspiration for Baz Lurhmann's student production of *Strictly Ballroom*.[53] His tradition was continued by Julia Cotton who succeeded him as Head of Movement Studies in 1995, and with Anca Frankenhaeuser ran the course until 2009. Subsequently, according to the students and professional observers, something uniquely valuable was lost. Students at NIDA who already have professional training in dance are scathing in their assessment.

The students of recent years have seen much evidence to justify their concerns. The graduating year of 2010 did not undertake a full play production until second term of second year and in the three years had only four productions, two of which were musicals. Over these years a sequence of external Artists-in-residence had been imposed by the Directorate, one of whom forced students to perform what was effectively a shouting match, to the alarm of their regular Acting and Voice teachers, who withdrew their students from the production. Another, imported for a Molière production, made no attempt to disguise his contempt for Australia's 'provincialism' and the poor quality of NIDA students.

This determination to overrule the Acting department in order to privilege other courses found students being subjected to cancellations of opening nights when, in one instance, scenery could not be properly operated; and in another, in an external venue, opening night became effectively a rehearsal because the scene shifters had installed the set back-to-front. The forward-planning demands made by designers and other heads through the Directorate have sometimes resulted in Acting teachers being pressured into casting students before they have had time to assess them. The teachers have resented this and students been disconcerted by it.

Another problem arising from the disruption of course structures were the changes enforced in the student assessment process. Indeed, at the end of 2011 the students became, in effect, collateral damage in the Director's assault on the Acting department. It was a well-established practice at the end of each NIDA year for all the relevant subject heads to discuss student assessments under the leadership of the Head of Acting. He was responsible for final/overall assessment of the students' achievement (pass/provisional pass/ fail), and a process of 'moderating' ensured balance and fairness. Students could pass/fail any one subject, but unless the subject was Acting itself (or the student was judged to be lacking in professional discipline) this did not determine the result for the whole year. All results were presented first to the Board of Examiners (chaired by Williams) and then to the Board of Studies for ratification.

By the end of 2011 Tony Knight was long gone and Kevin Jackson was on the outer—so much so that Andrew Ross, Head of Music, was appointed Interim Head of Acting. The end-of-year assessment for acting students was signed off by a staff member who was not an acting teacher and who had had no direct responsibility for setting or teaching the acting course itself. When these assessments reached the Board of Studies, members queried this process and were informed that Jackson had agreed with, or in effect signed off on, the assessments before his departure. Jackson made no such assessment and this information given to the Board of Studies was not correct. Complaints to Chairman Long were met with a response of masterful obfuscation which described the assessment process as being 'made cumulatively on a weighted task by task basis by the relevant teaching staff working together' and on the basis of advice of '*all* relevant members of the Acting Department'.[54]

Fundraising exercises like the Open Program, and hiring of the theatres, have also on occasion taken precedence over students' needs for rehearsal and performance space. In the words of the *Sydney Morning Herald*'s Garry Maddox, quoting a NIDA source:

> *They [the students] don't have access to rehearsal rooms out of hours because those are being turned over to open program activities teaching junior bank managers how to make better PowerPoint presentations.*[55]

The Parade Theatre was purpose built for the use and training of NIDA students but is also a major fundraiser for NIDA with external hirers. A number of recent NIDA productions have been mounted in the drafty caverns of Carriageworks on the pretext that working outside the NIDA comfort zone will develop student skills. A space built specifically for NIDA students is increasingly hired out to commercial operators, to the exclusion of the resident students.

When Peter Cooke was Deputy Director, up to ten members of NIDA staff were present to observe technical rehearsals for major student productions. Their presence guaranteed input from all parts of the school. These days it is not uncommon for that number to be down to one or two. The former Directors also took part in student auditions, were major assessors of final year productions before they were seen by the public and assisted students in the critical task of preparing their major presentation pieces for Agent's Day.[56] But no longer.

Most of all, every NIDA student's fear is not to secure an Agent on graduation. Many past students have had the luxury of picking their own Agent from among those on offer. For others it's a hard slog. Historically, Directors or senior Acting teachers would swing into action after Agents' Day and their long experience ensured that no graduate was left without an agent. Will a Director without this experience, and a newly arrived foreign Head of Acting, be able to provide this essential service in 2012?

10

The Board

This is where the buck stops.

NIDA is a public company limited by guarantee and operates under the provisions of the *Corporations Act 2001*. It is charged (inter alia) with the responsibility to 'maintain and enhance the Company's role as a centre of excellence in the performing arts' and must 'recognise the need to monitor the educational and artistic performance of the Company'.[57]

It has a membership (shareholders) and the NIDA Board has the unqualified right to determine this number at any time—currently 50. Membership of the Company is effectively awarded at the invitation of the Board, although there are provisions for individuals to apply. There are no qualifications for membership, such as donation or fundraising (in fact the most generous donors are not members) and members are not required to advance or support NIDA's activities in any way. Membership is for a period of seven years with a right to apply to the Board (in its absolute discretion) for a further five-year period. Beyond those 12 years further renewals are possible at the discretion of the Board. Membership of the NIDA Company confers only two benefits: the right to vote at meetings of the Company (including the AGM at which the Board is elected) and invitations to performances presented by NIDA students. Members of the Company are not asked to *do* anything specifically and generally fewer than eight bother to attend the only Company meeting of the year, the AGM.[58]

Access to membership is therefore very much a matter in the control of the Board of the day. Take the case of Terence Clarke, theatre director and long-standing teacher at NIDA, joint writer (with Nick Enright) of the musical *The Venetian Twins*, and a man of consummate knowledge of Australian theatre. Clarke applied for membership when the number of Company members was 42. Despite repeated assurances from the Chairman that his nomination would be brought forward for consideration by the Board, this was never done. More than a year after his application was made, and after repeated requests by him to the Chair, he was informed that the NIDA membership was now full and his application could not be considered. However, in the interim eight members had been added to the NIDA Company, favoured candidates of the Board. The Board could have increased the membership. It chose not to. Clarke had been a critic of the new regime.

Members of the NIDA Board of Directors serve a three-year term, with a limit of two consecutive terms.[59] The NIDA Constitution provides that the Board shall consist of between five and fifteen members (currently there are thirteen) of whom one must be a nominee of the University of NSW, one of the SBWF, with the Director and the Chair of the Board of Studies ex-officio. The Board is virtually self-selecting. Here are three examples, beginning with my own experience.

I was approached to serve on the NIDA Board after my retirement in 1990 from the Parliament where I had been the federal Shadow Minister for the Arts. My tenure was 1991–6 and I found it a stimulating and rewarding environment where my interest in all aspects of NIDA's work was welcomed and encouraged. After leaving the Board I maintained an active interest in NIDA and by 2007 had become concerned by the then Board's apparent lack of direction. I resolved to nominate independently for election at the next Annual General Meeting and was initially advised that my application would be supported. However, Company members were in due course advised that

> with input from an external search firm, the candidates were ranked according to how they best met the assessed needs of the Board. Mr Puplick was not ranked sufficiently for endorsement by the Board.

One does learn some things in politics. No doubt to the chagrin of some, I turned up on the day with ten supporters in attendance and holding 19 proxy votes (29 out of a maximum of 50). The Board folded, and in order to curtail the chance of my using my 29 votes to wipe out the retiring members of the Board and reject the new nominees, passed a special resolution to invite me to join the Board.

It has long been a criticism of the NIDA Board that it lacks adequate representation from the theatre profession itself. Beside the Director and Chair, the 2011 Board consisted of two management consultants, a lawyer, a television executive, two academics, a film maker, an advertising executive, an interior designer, one actor and one theatre producer. Of these, one is based in Melbourne, one in New Zealand and one elsewhere overseas. In 2012 the actor, interior designer and film maker were replaced by a theatre director, a company director and another lawyer.

In 2010 two established NIDA graduates, actor/producer Felix Williamson and screenwriter/playwright Nick Parsons were persuaded by the staff to nominate for the Board. There were vacancies, so their addition would not have displaced any existing members. Both were rejected on the existing Board's recommendation. In 2011 graduate and actor Tony Llewellyn-Jones sought election. Again there were vacancies, again he was rejected. One who was added, however, was Judith Isherwood, Chief Executive of the Arts Centre, Melbourne. In her first year on the Board she attended only two of the six board meetings held and did not attend the AGM.[60] In that year a further two Directors managed to attend only three of the six meetings held.

Another factor that weakened the Board's familiarity with NIDA's affairs was the management decision to exclude Board members from attendance at anything other than public performances. Successive Chairs Dame Leonie Kramer, Rod McGeogh and Len Mauger in their time had actively encouraged the Board to attend as many student performances and presentations as possible. These included not only the public presentations but the internal showings, the small-scale presentation pieces and the Acting 2 students' personal 'movement pieces'. In addition Board members were invited to observe both auditions and rehearsals and to develop an understanding of the crafts involved.

This was another practice of old NIDA to be eliminated. Board members were now excluded from attendance at anything other than public performances.

The matter came to a head when Williams and Long decided to make the decision into a Board ruling. I sought legal opinion which confirmed that a Board Director had the right to inform him/herself of the full range of school activities, provided this did not interfere with the running of the school and was done with the permission of the teachers/students involved. The Chair then produced a contrary legal opinion (not from NIDA's regular solicitors, but externally at a cost to NIDA of some $9,600). That opinion stated:

> *It is the board (as a whole) who is required to recognise the need to monitor the educational and artistic performance of NIDA. It would not be possible for the directors to carry out that function unless they had appropriate opportunity to view performances by the* students and other operational aspects of NIDA. *However unlimited access for these purposes is impractical and inappropriate.*
> [My emphasis]

On this basis the NIDA Board determined that access for any Board member to any non-public event at NIDA would be entirely at the discretion of the Director, and could be effected only by seeking her permission in writing. Every single request made by me for access (following invitations from staff and students) to view any of these non-public events was refused.

The extent to which the NIDA Board allowed itself to have its right of access to student activities reduced to that of the general public must call into question the extent to which its members are capable of discharging the monitoring duty imposed upon them by the NIDA Constitution. Yet even this minimum requirement has appeared too much for some NIDA Board members. Some have attended none of the year's activities, others only one or two of the final works in the third-year program.

I am concerned at the extent to which the Board members engage in a regular assessment of the school's educational and artistic achievements. My own experience was that in over the last three years of service we had no significant presentation or discussion of such matters at any Board meeting. Nor did the Director bring an assessment or invite discussion on the progress of the students. In my previous six years on the Board these had been led by Clark and were especially required by the Chair, Dame Leonie Kramer. While others may argue that such an assessment is the responsibility of the Board of Studies, even their reports to the main Board were of an entirely technical and regulatory nature.

In 2009 Egon Zehnder International undertook a review of the effectiveness of the NIDA Board of Directors.[61] They interviewed all members of the

Board. Among their findings were that:

- only 50% (of Directors) felt the relationship between the CEO and the Directors was 'appropriate and healthy';
- The lack of focus of Board agendas was highlighted with 58% 'undecided or disagree that Agendas are effective';
- 58% felt that too little time was devoted to fundraising, revenue and future strategies or staff/student development;
- only 50% or less of the board agree or strongly agree that: the strategy is clearly articulated and understood; the Board concurs fully with the strategy; there is an effective strategic planning and review process in place; the organisation has the right balance between short and long term goals; the organisation is fully capturing strategic opportunities.

In any Board there are bound to be disagreements, especially when doubts arise about the management. However, the NIDA Board's response has been in effect to regard almost any dissent as unacceptable.

The role of the dissident director is a problematic one. Corporation law professor Bob Baxt writes that directors have a clear responsibility to be more than mere ornaments. He describes a case in which a Board of Directors was responsible for the operations of a service station. The courts found several of them negligent because

> *they took no steps to inform themselves of the affairs of the company, become familiar with the business or understand how the business was generally run.*

He notes that courts have held that there was almost a public 'duty' in directors informing shareholders 'of what was going on in the boardroom despite the confidentiality obligations of directors' since the primary duty of any director is to the shareholders and not the Board.[62]

Elizabeth Knight in the *Sydney Morning Herald* argued (in relation to a case involving a company takeover about which one director was seeking more information) that while 'this may be particularly irritating for the remaining directors' it was nevertheless vital to the effective operation of the Board as a whole. The Board had a responsibility, she added, to declare to shareholders 'the position of all directors including the person who holds some doubts'.[63]

Another *SMH* writer, Fiona Shand, put it more bluntly:

> *We need boardrooms to be places where collegiality does not trump independence. Good governance practices demand intelligent directors with inquiring minds, a diverse range of expertise, skills and experience who are not bound by collegiate decision-making or patronage.*[64]

Justin Macdonnell, one of our most successful theatre entrepreneurs, has been even more critical in relation to Arts Boards: filling the boards of arts companies with business and legal appointees has 'stifled creativity' and led to a situation in which it was becoming questionable as to 'whether the boards had the capacity to choose good artistic leadership'.[65]

Elizabeth Butcher, in reflecting on some forty years of major involvement in theatre and arts boards observed that an 'ideal board' should 'accept more responsibility for artistic excellence in addition to performing their fiscal and legal responsibilities', have greater artistic representation on them and above all recognise that the roles of artistic director and general manager should never be vested in the one person because 'the jobs are fundamentally different, and so time-consuming they require very different sets of knowledge and practical skills'. She also added that, in relation to her tenure at NIDA, she and the Director

> *kept the NIDA Board well-informed on all artistic and educational issues [...] especially the artistic and educational rationale underpinning all management changes.*[66]

Comparing the performance of the NIDA Boards of recent years against such criteria I consider that they come off distinctly second-rate. Here is what I have observed:

- Dissident directors were uniformly cold-shouldered and indeed both Clark and myself were asked to leave the Board, under threat of being forcibly removed for failure to give unqualified support to Williams, and were followed in protest by two others. Clark resigned before the expiry of his term (he had been invited to join it in 2006, two years after his retirement), after writing to Company members that 'clearly my knowledge and experience is not valued by the board'.

- The Board's failure to respond to the mass dismissals/sackings/departures of almost all the senior staff over a relatively short period, and a turnover of over 30% in some departments within a year, must itself raise questions about the extent to which the Board is briefed on the changes within NIDA.

- The rejection of all attempts by NIDA graduates

and theatre practitioners to be considered for membership of the Board, and the perceived patronage of other placements has been derisory and adds force to Justin Macdonnell's concerns about their ability to make an appropriate choice of artistic leadership.

• The demand that collegiality take absolute precedence over the exercise of independent judgement is, in my view, not an exemplar of good governance in practice.

Bryce Hallett in the *SMH*, observing the increasing corporatisation of NIDA in 2010, was moved to describe it as

a management model more characterised by private consultancy, myriad committees, outsourcing and a marketing department in overdrive to protect the school's image,

and a staff member to assert in print that: 'The Board is a marionette theatre with enough puppets to make the real actors not matter.'[67]

There is a need for greater transparency. Under Elizabeth Butcher, minutes of all Board meetings were lodged in the Library for any member of staff to inspect. No longer. Requests by myself to attend a briefing given to all staff by the Chairman and the Chair of the Board of Studies to talk about the current thinking of the Board in October 2009 was refused.

Long has given unqualified support to Williams throughout her tenure and must shoulder much of the responsibility for what has occurred at NIDA. Described by broadcasting historian K. S. Inglis as 'a cautious inhabitant of the Australian public sphere' and 'short on vitality', with a tendency to 'lecture',[68] Long has been particularly supportive of Williams' corporatist approach to redefining the NIDA 'brand', having himself written in support of having a Brand Australia Council 'to effectively position and brand Australia in the global marketplace.'[69] As Executive Director of AFTRS, he was responsible for the appointment of Sandra Levy as chief executive, whose tenure has been marked by many similar problems and issues as has Williams'. While I do not subscribe to the maxim 'if it ain't broke don't fix it', I believe that if you inherit a model which has produced the finest acting, design and related theatre graduates, been the mainstay of the Australian theatre, television and movie industry for decades and recognised as one of the world's leading theatre schools and institutions, you don't spit on its legacy, demean its practitioners, decimate its staff and think that you've done your job, like Tacitus—*solitudinem faciunt pacem appellant.*[70]

11

The old order changeth, yielding place to new

And so it should. It is arguable that Clark and Butcher should have retired earlier and that no teaching institution should fail to steadily renew at the very top, especially in such a changing technological and educational environment. However, a financially and administratively strong organisation, universally respected and producing graduates in all disciplines of the highest calibre, is not something to be casually discarded. The advent of Malcolm Long, a man whose record suggests more interest in structures than content, and Lynne Williams, a woman with no appropriate experience and with a Thatcherite style honed after a quarter of a century in the UK, has meant that NIDA can never be the same again.[72]

Of course it could be better. But successful reinvigoration depends on explaining and championing a change agenda which is clear, articulate, pedagogically and theatrically based, justified, respectful of NIDA's past and embraced by those staff who would be on the front line of its delivery. Unfortunately, in this instance, the centre of gravity shifted from the stage to the office.

Vladimir Nemirovich-Danchenko, writing of the establishment of the Moscow Art Theatre, observed:

> *The office should yield precedence to the demands of the stage. The theatre exists for that which happens on the stage, for the creativeness of the actor and author, and not for those who manage them. The office must resiliently accommodate itself to all the curves, unexpectedness, collisions, which fill the atmosphere of artistic labour.*[73]

NIDA is not a theatre company, but a training school but I believe the same principles apply.[74]

What staff wanted after Mellor's unhappy departure was the fulfilment of those promises made of bringing them an artistic leader who was a genuine industry professional, supported by a competent general manager. Most of them have felt betrayed that they got neither. Among the industry generally a feeling grew that NIDA's pre-eminence was slipping, not just because WAAPA was growing strongly,[75] that other actor-training opportunities were opening up in Sydney[76] and that the VCA was reviving because, as Ros Walker put it:

> *We now have a dean who is a respected practitioner, and who is going to be sympathetic to the way in which artists are trained,*[77]

but because the Director did not have the language to talk with the artistic and educational staff; so the fear of dumbing-down became pervasive.[78] Staff turnover suggests that NIDA is not a happy place, that morale is low; and concerns about the way in which key staff have departed and the effective destruction of NIDA's corporate memory are the talk of many a theatre foyer.

At the same time, the Director's Centre for Contemporary Performance Practice is an unlikely prospect, not because it is a bad idea, quite the contrary—although one can debate how academic, rather than practically-based, NIDA should become[79]—but simply because there is at present so little prospect of the Federal Government financing it.

It need not, should not, have been so. The Director should have had the skills to manage better, to understand better the artistic temperament, and even to believe that there was an Australian competent enough to be appointed as Head of Acting. Throughout these conflicts, I felt the Board went AWOL and was found missing in action. Richard Murphet's study of the VCA contains this poignant observation:

> *For Lindy Davies, whose bailiwick was the actual training of artists, this bureaucratic shift deprived the training programs of power and undermined their effectiveness:*

[...] 'During the '80s, when all the artists were forced underground, the bureaucrats weren't underground; they were forming a culture that didn't need us.'[80]

So it has come to pass at NIDA. Most of the artists have left the building.

So, what is to be done?

In the first instance I believe that NIDA should be subjected to an external review, by respected educational and industry leaders, in much the same way as has happened recently at WAAPA, but unlike that exercise, focus should be not upon finance but upon issues of governance and pedagogy. I believe that the Australian Government, as NIDA's principal funder, should recognise that they have a problem and take steps to address it. A review commissioned and appointed internally will not do and will have no credibility. I call on the Federal Minister for the Arts to act before it is too late.

At the grass roots there is a need for the members of the NIDA Company to take their responsibilities seriously. The number of Company members should be expanded, the current closed-shop of Board appointments ended and membership open to those who wish to apply, like most organisations. Annual General Meetings should be made meaningful in terms of discussion of the Company's direction and objectives, and the Chair's practice of denying access to the media should be ended.[81] NIDA, operating primarily with public money, must be transparent.

The Board must introduce more members with real educational and theatrical experience to balance the legal and financial expertise; and give thought to reviving the practice of electing a staff and a student representative to the Board. They must be vigilant about standards and engage in robust debates about NIDA's artistic policies and outcomes; and the Chair must accept that dissent is not treason but can be a spur to better practice.

The Board must also resolve that Lynne Williams' successor as Director will be, as was previously promised, a respected and leading member of the profession with the skills of an artist and a teacher; that these fields should be the Director's principal focus and that a general manager with separate responsibilities be again appointed.

Meanwhile, whether the 'new NIDA' will continue to lead theatre training and produce the stars and the industry leaders of the future; whether its artistic standards will continue to be what others aspire to emulate; whether it will take the lead in engagement with Indigenous Australia and Asia; and whether it will continue to deserve the respect it has earned from the Australian theatre and educational professions, remains an open question.

Endnotes

1   James Waites: *Whatever Happened to the STC Actors Company?* Sydney: Currency House, Platform Papers 23, April 2010.

2   Richard Murphet, *The Fall and Rise of the VCA*. Sydney: Currency House, Platform Papers 28, July 2011.

3   'Creative transformation' was a slogan sprung on the NIDA Board at a planning day in 2009 after being 'workshopped' by the new Director and an advertising agency. The Board had no hand in its development and even less understanding of its meaning.

4   Murphet: op cit p.7.

5   Long has an extensive background in broadcasting and film, at the ABC, SBS, AFTRS and as a member of the Australian Government's Convergence Review. K. S. Inglis: *Whose ABC ?* Melbourne: Black Ink, 2006.

6   Thomas Oliver: *The Real Coke, the Real Story,* New York: Penguin 1986.

7   John Clark: *NIDA* Sydney: DCITA and UNSW, 2003.

8   Geoffrey Dutton: *Snow on the Saltbush*, Ringwood: Viking, 1984 p.18.

9   Clark: op cit p. 21.

10 The Commonwealth provided some $9.2million of NIDA's budget of $18.1million in 2011 and owns the NIDA buildings which stand on land leased from UNSW.

11 These are the terms used in an email from Mellor to Broadbent.

12 Petition had dozens of signatories, including John Bell, Judy Davis, Colin Friels, Michael Gow, George Miller, Robyn Nevin, Geoffrey Rush, Fred Schepisi, Hugo Weaving. Valerie Lawson: 'Cate, Baz and Mel hold no sway', *Sydney Morning Herald,* 15 April 2008. Malcolm Chaikin, a former NIDA Chair, wrote publicly in support of Mellor, *Sydney Morning Herald*, 10 March 2008.

13 Rupert Myer: *Report of the Contemporary Visual arts and Crafts Inquiry* (2002); and the Senate (2007) report *Indigenous Art—Securing the Future: Australia's Indigenous visual arts and craft sector.*

14 NIDA: *Submission to the National Cultural Policy*, October 2011, accessed at www.culture.arts.gov.au.

15 Nicky McWilliam: 'Universities are letting Australian art down', *Sydney Morning Herald*, 24 March 2011.

16 Terry Cutler, *Venturous Australia—building strength in innovation*. Melbourne: Cutler & Co., 2008 p.50.

17 I do not know which institutions, domestic or international, were chosen. No report back on this exercise was made to the Board for discussion.

18 Valeria Lawson, 'Much ado about NIDA's direction', *Sydney Morning Herald*, 15–16 March 2008.

19 Malcolm Long, 'Statement to staff and students', 5 December 2007.

20 Joyce Morgan, 'NIDA casts about for a director', *Sydney Morning Herald*, 11 December 2007.

21 Valerie Lawson: loc cit.

22 Now Professor, Head School of Drama, Carnegie Mellon University.

23 Qualifications: DSCM (Sydney Conservatorium of Music) MA (University of Wollongong) Honorary Master of Letters (De Montfort University).

24 There was already before the Government a submission from Butcher for funding of NIDA Stage 3, based on a Business Case prepared by Public Assets P/L (11.11.2005) which included funding for new courses and a postgraduate school, together with a new building to accommodate them. Both Ministers Coonan and Brandis indicated support in principle for additional funding but this ceased with the election of the Rudd Labor Government, at which point Opposition Leader Nelson and Shadow Arts Minister Stone committed to support of NIDA Stage 3 to the tune of $6 million.

25 Australian Universities Quality Agency: *Report on an*

Audit of the National Institute of Dramatic Art, July 2010 pp. 10–11.

26   NIDA: *Annual Report*: 2008 p.5, 2009 p.5, 2010 p.5, 2011 p.5.

27   *Proverbs* 29.18.

28   These include revisions to the Directors' course and the introduction of Playwriting and Masters' courses—all of which were under development under Clark. The Graduate Diploma and Masters' courses in Playwriting had received accreditation but were not funded.

29   In comparing staffing lists 2008 and 2012 one sees the departure of 3 of 5 Heads of Courses; 4 of 6 Heads of Departments; 4 of 6 Acting Staff; 3 of 4 Library; 17 of 23 Development; 3 of 3 Sponsorship; 11 of 18 Operations; 4 of 4 Archives; 1 of 3 Accounts; 7 of 9 Administration.

30   Each of these personal case studies appears with the consent of the principal concerned and all emails quoted are in my possession. The interpretation is my own.

31   Taken from Roberts' paper, 'Comments regarding the draft report on the Rodney Seaborn Library, May-June 2009'.

32   Lyn Pierse: *Improvisation—The Guide,* Sydney: Empire Publishing, 3rd ed. 2007.

33   Joe Hildebrand: 'Enter, stage fright', *Daily Telegraph*, 15 August 2009.

34   See Terence Crawford: *Trade Secrets—Australian actors and their craft,* Sydney: Currency Press, 2005; Terence Crawford: *Dimensions of Acting—An Australian Approach,* Sydney: Currency Press, 2011.

35   David Malouf: *A Spirit of Play,* Boyer Lectures 1998, Sydney: ABC Books, 2001.

36   See Michel Saint-Denis: *Theatre: The Rediscovery of Style and Other Writings,* ed. Jane Baldwin, London: Routledge, 2009.

37   Tony Knight liked to describe the style as based on Shakespeare's injunction:

> *The poet's eye, in fine frenzy rolling*
> *Doth glance from heaven to earth, from earth to heaven*
> *And as imagination bodies forth*
> *The form of things unknown, the poet's pen*
> *Turns them to shapes and gives to airy nothing*
> *A local habitation and a name.*
>
> *A Midsummer Night's Dream* v.1.12–17.

38 Especially his warning, 'you should not hurry to get on the stage and try to act, physically and emotionally, too soon'. Saint-Denis: op cit p.66. Clearly not Jeff Janisheski's approach.

39 www.theoneill.org/national-theatre-institute/nti-semester.

40 NIDA: *NIDA News* Vol 29, December 2011 p.12.

41 NIDA Media Release: *NIDA Appoints new Head of Acting*, 3 November 2011. Revealingly, this press release ends with a tag line that this recruitment was done 'with the support of Braithwaite Steiner Pretty'.

42 Jeff was good enough to grant me an extended and generous interview for this Paper, despite knowing my general view of NIDA's recent history and doubtless being aware of the tensions in the Acting Department and the School prior to his appointment.

43 In relation to Shakespeare, Janisheski has indicated in his 'Learning Outcomes' notes to students that apart from stopping 'speaking in a classical voice', they need to 'avoid the Shakespeare police'.

44 See Hilary Glow and Katya Johanson: *Your Genre is Black: Indigenous performing arts and policy.* Sydney: Currency House, Platform Papers 19, January 2009; Lee Lewis: *Cross-racial Casting: Changing the face of Australian theatre,* Sydney: Currency House, Platform Papers 13, July 2007.

45 Alison Carroll and Carrillo Gantner: *Finding a Place on the Asian Stage.* Sydney: Currency House, Platform Papers 31, April 2012.

46 Bernard Lane: 'Henry issues call for Asia study', *Weekend Australian,* 14–15 July 2012.

47   Aubrey Mellor: 'Notes from Playbox' in *Blak Inside*: 6 *Indigenous Plays from Victoria,* Sydney: Currency Press 2002; Hilary Glow: 'Recent Indigenous Theatre in Australia' *International Journal of the Humanities*, vol.4 (1) 2006.

48   Bryce Hallett: 'Once more unto the breach', *Sydney Morning Herald*, June 12–13, 2010.

49   Keith Gallasch: 'Theatre/Performance Education: Home and the World', Sydney: *Real Time 104* August/September, *105* October/November 2011.

50   Tim Elliott: 'Drama School takes TV money', *Sydney Morning Herald,* 10 November 2010.

51   I have a copy of the survey and have interviewed students involved in its conduct.

52   Keith Bain: *Keith Bain on Movement,* ed. Michael Campbell, Sydney: Currency House, 2010. Keith died in July 2012 as this paper was being written.

53   Itself an international success primarily due to Butcher's entrepreneurial skills in funding its development at a critical juncture.

54   Emphasis added. I have copies of the relevant correspondence but of course protect the identity of the parties.

55   Garry Maddox: 'Dramas of the wrong kind', *Sydney Morning Herald*, 31 October 2010.

56   This is the student's final presentation at NIDA when they appear in individual pieces (which are also on a show reel) before an audience of theatre Agents. Securing a good Agent is vital to the success of any actor, so this is the most critical performance of their three years at NIDA. The role of previous directors in making sure the students were seen at their best was absolutely critical.

57   NIDA Constitution, sections 42.3 and 42.4.

58   Excluding those Company members who are directors.

59   In 2010 Bruce Cutler was restored to the Board for a further three years after having completed two consecutive terms (2003–9) and after only a one-year absence.

60 NIDA: *Annual Report 2011* p.32.
61 Egon Zehnder International: 'National Institute of Dramatic Art—review of the effectiveness of the Board of Directors', June 2009.
62 Bob Baxt: *Duties and Responsibilities of Directors and Officers*, Sydney: Australian Institute of Company Directors,19th ed. 2009 p.96.
63 Elizabeth Knight: 'Value of a dissenting director at the table', *Sydney Morning Herald*, 17 November 2010.
64 Fiona Shand: 'Diversity the answer for boardrooms', *Sydney Morning Herald*, 9 May 2012.
65 Quoted in Joyce Morgan: 'Business-like arts a failure, says entrepreneur', *Sydney Morning Herald*, 3 April 2009.
66 Elizabeth Butcher: 'Towards an Ideal Board', address to Currency House Arts and Public Life Breakfast, Sydney, 25 March 2009.
67 Hallett: loc cit.
68 Inglis, K. S., *Whose ABC?* Collingwood, Victoria: Black Inc., 2006 p.449.
69 Malcolm Long, 'Rebranding Australia', *The Drum Opinion* 5 February 2012.
70 Where they make a desert they call it peace.
71 Tennyson: *Idylls of the King* (1869) l. 408.
72 Michael Billington: *State of the Nation—British theatre since 1945*, London: Faber & Faber, 2007.
73 Vladimir Nemirovish-Danchenko: *My Life in the Russian Theatre*, Michigan: Theatre Art Books, University of Michigan, 2010 p.89–90.
74 This dilemma was highlighted in the recent *WAAPA Review* (A Review commissioned by Edith Cowan University from Prof Peter Matthews, 30 May 2012) which was critical of WAAPA's institutionalised 'over-teaching' and the 'unresolved internal debate on the balance between its roles as "Educational Institution" and "Production Company"' in the end stressing that 'The capacity to produce "in-house" performances for, with and by students is WAAPA's greatest peda-

gogical strength but they must respond primarily to educational rather than arts management imperatives.' (Review p. vii).

75 Victoria Laurie: 'All cacophonous on the Western front', *Australian*, 17 June 2010.

76 Dean Carey's Actors Centre continues to expand and prosper; Bell Shakespeare is running actor training courses (see *Sydney Morning Herald* 30 July 2012) and an International Screen Academy of Sydney, specialising in actor training for film, television and electronic media is on the cards.

77 Murphet: op cit p.56.

78 Maddox: loc cit.

79 This issue has not been explored in any depth by either of the reports commissioned on the CCPP by Fiona Winning (June 2009) or Root Projects P/L (March 2010), although the Director has suggested that models such as Middlesex University's Centre for Research into Creation in the Performing Arts or Brunel University's Centre for Contemporary and Digital Performance are relevant.

80 Murphet: op cit p. 21.

81 In 2010 the journalist Adam Fulton was barred by the Chair from attending the AGM and asked to leave. *Sydney Morning Herald*, 'Exit, Stage Right', 26 May 2010.

Reader's Forum

Response to Clinton Walker, *History is Made at Night: Live music in Australia.*

SHANE HOMAN is a music industry and cultural policy researcher at Monash University. He is the co-author of two commissioned reports on the music industries in NSW and Victoria: *Vanishing Acts: an Inquiry into the State of Live Music Opportunities in NSW* (2003) and *The Music Capital: City of Melbourne Music Strategy* (2010).

On 13 August Michael Gudinski, founder of Mushroom Records, delivered the annual Thomas Rome lecture at the National Film and Sound Archives awards in Melbourne Town Hall. The Mushroom Group CEO was in good form, if extremely selective in terms of both personal and company histories (mythologising the good, excising the bad). Yet it was also a reminder of the passion of a major player in the growth of Australian rock and pop from the early 1970s. As Clinton Walker's essay states, Gudinski's original booking agency, Consolidated Rock, was crucial in establishing Victoria's live rock circuits before the formation of the Mushroom recording label.

For me, *History is Made at Night* reinforces the importance of passionate, unshakeable individuals in ensuring that cities have viable and meaningful live music scenes. This includes, of course, the author himself—Walker can rightfully claim a long history of intelligent writing about music that in many instances allowed mainstream Australia a glimpse of those working on the edges of respectability. One of several recurring themes in this essay is that if left to government, live music at night would consist of the touristic and the simplistic. Walker takes aim at several organisations found wanting in battles to preserve music venue infrastructure. Some of this criticism is valid, such as that of the Musicians'

Union. Other criticism is not; for example, APRA, the peak collection society, has been very active behind the scenes in negotiation at both state and federal levels of government.

Walker also reminds us that successful music cities are ecosystems: venues can't survive on their own, but remain dependent upon good booking promoters and agencies, music education networks and innovative media networks (the contributions of radio stations RRR and PBS in Melbourne are instructive here, and the enthusiastic street music press). In the case of Sydney in 2012, it's back to the future: the revival of town hall and bowling club gigs provides a lifeline for non-mainstream scenes.

This essay is a good primer for those unfamiliar with various state debates and activity: where punters and musicians see crucibles of innovation and community, governments merely see public assembly and amenity issues. Some of the venue battles here are overly simplified and point to a wider range of issues and the complexity of individual venues and scenes. The parcels of real estate upon which local music venues are situated are now so valuable that residential redevelopment seems almost inevitable. Walker speaks of this, the fleeting nature of many venues, and the exceptions that are of twenty or thirty years' standing. This also speaks to the continuing effort to recognise the live music experience as one of cultural significance. While we don't want iconic venues to be sprayed with the heritage gloss that renders them as the plastic experiences so often found in the United States, the value of the individual gig to transform our understanding of a band, a genre or a scene has to be grounded more solidly in the cultural soil.

As one who has contributed to the 'piles of publicly funded paper' on live music, the current debates about the levels of Australia Council and other funding for the high arts are, of course not unrelated to the live music debate. The Trainor/James review of the Australia Council delivered in May 2012 acknowledged the need for contemporary music to be brought fully into the funding tent; and the need for live music to be similarly recognised beyond its commercial imperatives. This is part of a set of wider discussions about how OzCo now sees the popular as an important part of the national cultural furniture.

Whether we like it or not, what is self-evident within popular music communities must be continually demonstrated to governments who often remain in ignorance of the mixture of cultural, political and social issues involved. Where Walker despairs at the number of commissioned reports stating the same case on regulation and the economic worth of live music, there has been progress. The move by most states to new liquor licence categories based upon risk and behaviour histories will in the long term assist the small music venue, along with the small bar licence revival in several states. Where other measures may fail, recent reports revealing the economic worth of live music are more than useful in bringing other issues to the government table. As Walker notes, the inequities in noise law remain the central issue, particularly in Victoria, where the push is on to introduce 'order of occupancy'/ 'agent of change' regulations that can protect existing venues from resident complaints.

As has been noted in other public forums, two important test cases loom in Melbourne. The Cherry Bar on AC/DC Lane in the CBD, and the Corner Hotel in Richmond, both contend with nearby apartment developments under construction. For all the encouraging words from government about respecting music venues in their cultural and industrial forms, if either iconic venue is forced to change their current trading hours or music activity to accommodate their new neighbours, what the state really thinks about liveability indexes and the role of the 'cultural city' will be made decidedly clear.

FORTHCOMING

PP34: January 2013
IT'S CULTURE, STUPID!
Leigh Tabrett

In 2005, with a lifelong interest in the arts, a career background in higher education and no professional experience of arts administration, Leigh Tabrett was appointed to lead the Queensland Government's arts agency. She was also chair of the Cultural Ministers' Council Statistics Working Group and has contributed to the development of the Australian Government's forthcoming National Cultural Policy. In a trenchant examination of her years in those roles she explores how the lack of clarity about the core purposes of government funding has reached deep into how these systems operate both at State and Federal level. Can we have a national system of public support, she asks, in the absence of a clear sense of purpose for such a system?

Is there a better way?

AT YOUR LOCAL BOOKSHOP FROM 15 JANUARY
AND AS A PAPERBACK OR ELECTRONICALLY
FROM OUR WEBSITE AT
WWW.CURRENCYHOUSE.ORG.AU